SOUTH FLORIDA

TEN THOUSAND ISLANDS

MIAMI

THE EVERGLADES

BISCAYNE BAY

PRESENT RANGE

SUITABLE HABITAT

GULF OF MEXICO

KEY LARGO

FLAMINGO

CAPE SABLE

ATLANTIC OCEAN

N

W E

S

FLORIDA BAY

THE FLORIDA KEYS

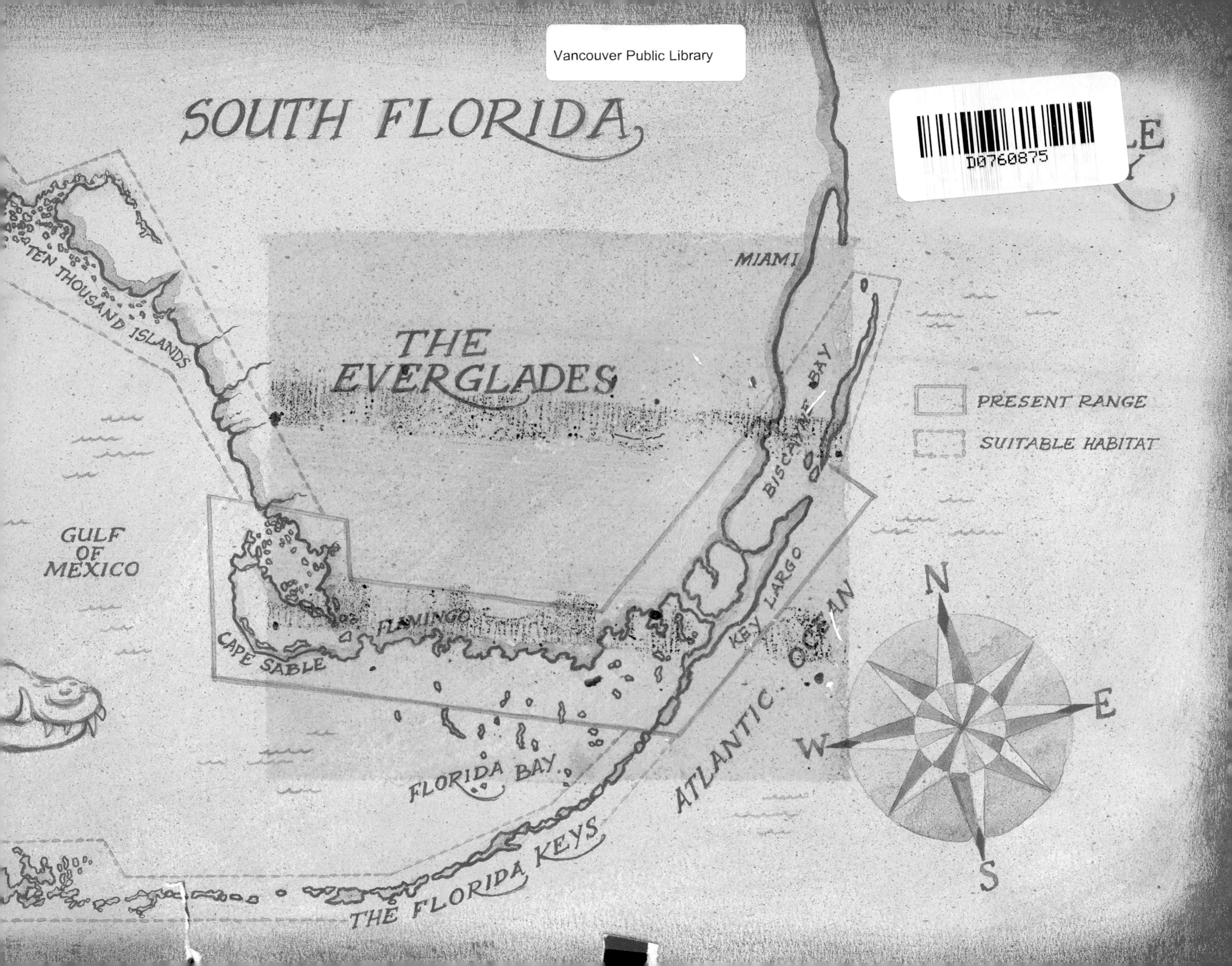

Crocodile Safari

This book is dedicated to Steve Klett, who works
every day on behalf of the American Crocodile.

Library of Congress Cataloging-in-Publication Data

Arnosky, Jim.
  Crocodile safari / Written and illustrated by Jim Arnosky.
    p. cm.
  ISBN-13: 978-0-439-90356-1 (hardcover)
  ISBN-10: 0-439-90356-4 (hardcover)
  1. Crocodiles—Juvenile literature. I. Title.
  QL666.C925A763 2009
  597.98'2—dc22

                    2008006954

10 9 8 7 6 5 4 3 2 1   09 10 11 12 13

Printed in Singapore   46
First edition, March 2009

The display type was set in You Are Loved and Chelt Press.
The text was set in Pabst and Journal.
The art was created using acrylic paint in a semi-translucent
  style on acid-free watercolor paper.
Book design by Becky Terhune

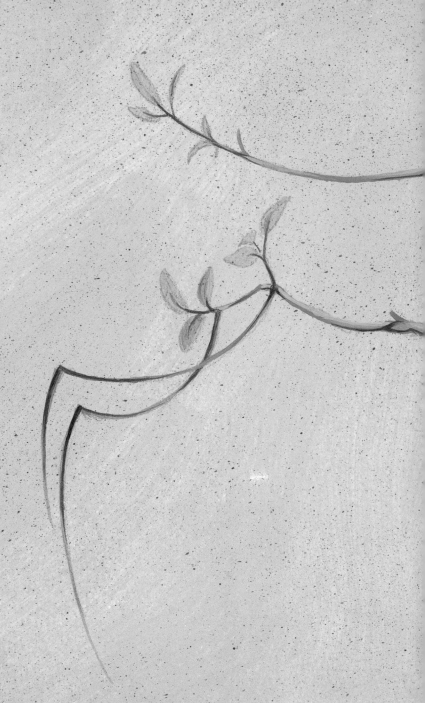

Crocodile Safari

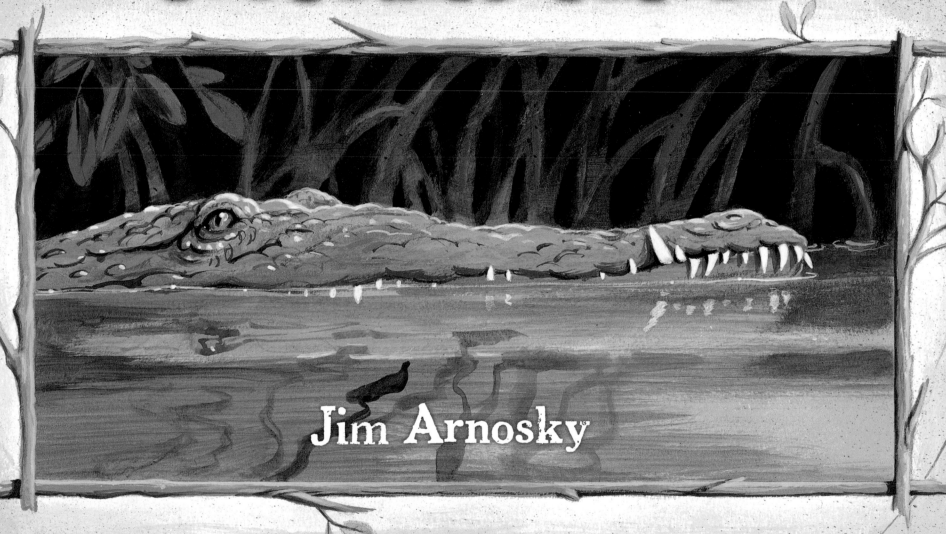

Jim Arnosky

Scholastic Press
New York

Jim and Deanna Arnosky exploring crocodile habitat

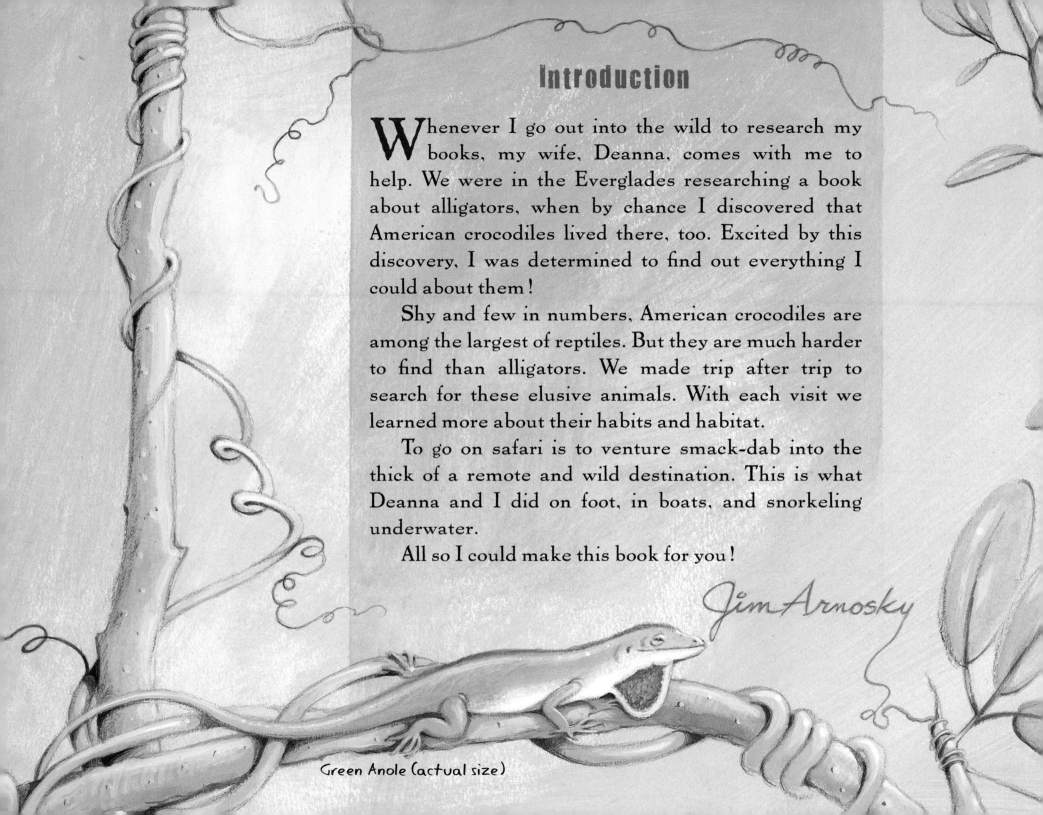

Introduction

Whenever I go out into the wild to research my books, my wife, Deanna, comes with me to help. We were in the Everglades researching a book about alligators, when by chance I discovered that American crocodiles lived there, too. Excited by this discovery, I was determined to find out everything I could about them!

Shy and few in numbers, American crocodiles are among the largest of reptiles. But they are much harder to find than alligators. We made trip after trip to search for these elusive animals. With each visit we learned more about their habits and habitat.

To go on safari is to venture smack-dab into the thick of a remote and wild destination. This is what Deanna and I did on foot, in boats, and snorkeling underwater.

All so I could make this book for you!

Jim Arnosky

Green Anole (actual size)

COUNTING CROCODILES

Canoeing slowly past a large wild crocodile is like paddling back in time to the age of the dinosaurs. Crocodiles have been around since prehistoric times. The American crocodile was classified as an endangered species. They had been overhunted. Development invaded their habitat. In the late twentieth century, there were fewer than 300 crocodiles left in the United States.

Since then, crocodiles have been protected by law.

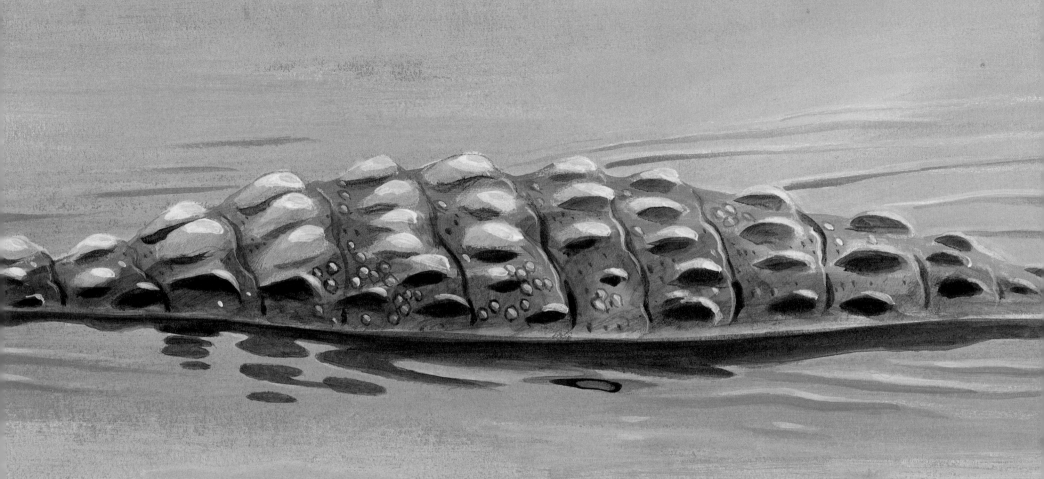

Most of their remaining habitat has been preserved. And today in the
United States, the American crocodile is no longer considered endangered.
Although it is still endangered in the rest of its range — Central America,
South America, Mexico, and the Caribbean.

There are now approximately 2,000 crocodiles in the United States.
How do we know? Somebody counted them while flying over their habitat!

On our safari, Deanna and I decided we would count all the crocodiles
we could find while exploring their habitat on water and land.

ALLIGATOR OR CROCODILE?

Before we set out to count, we needed to know how to tell a crocodile apart from an alligator. Here is what we discovered.

Alligators are mostly black in color. Crocodiles are tan when they are dry, and brown when they are wet. An alligator's snout is wide and broadly rounded at the tip. A crocodile's snout is tapered to a rounded point. Most of an alligator's teeth are hidden when the mouth is closed. Croc teeth show even when the mouth is closed. Alligators are primarily freshwater animals. Crocodiles prefer salt water.

Mangrove Cuckoo

When swimming, a crocodile's profile in the water is higher than that of an alligator.

Crocodile

Alligator

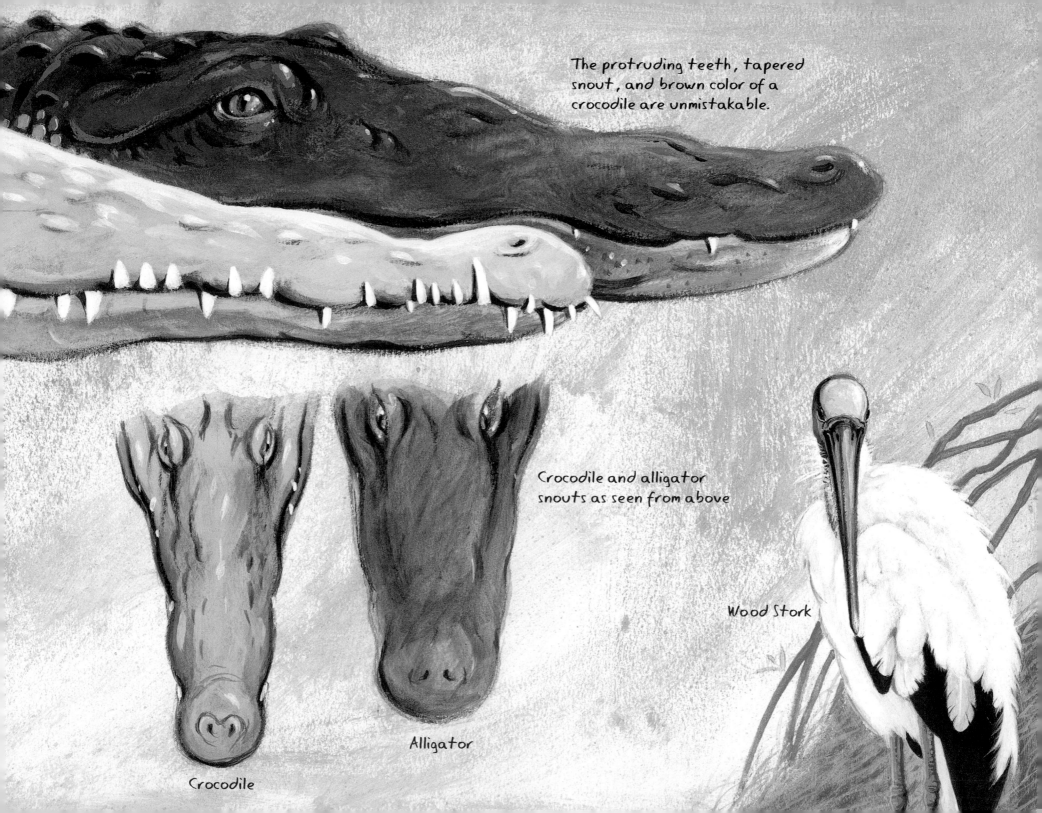

The protruding teeth, tapered snout, and brown color of a crocodile are unmistakable.

Crocodile and alligator snouts as seen from above

Wood Stork

Crocodile

Alligator

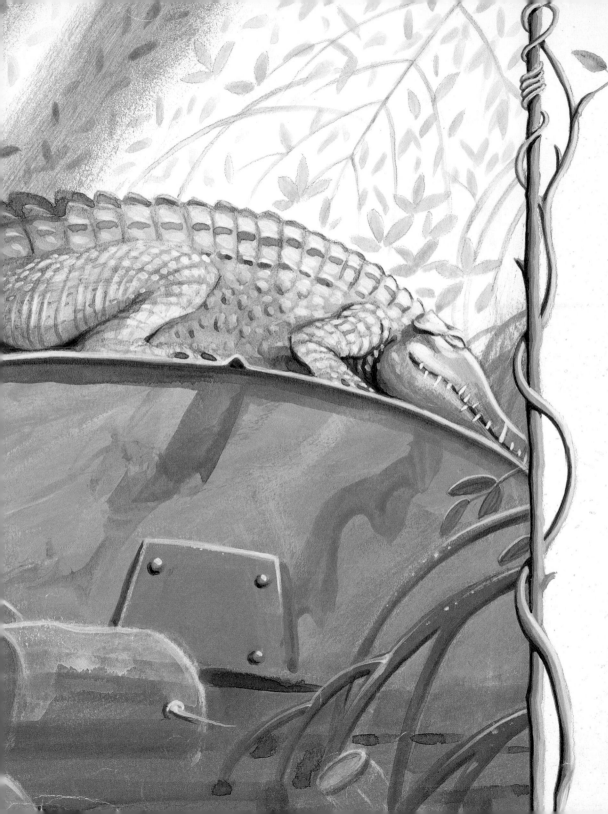

JUNKYARD DINOSAURS

The first wild crocodiles we found were in a very unlikely place. It was a trash-filled mangrove creek that flowed through a trailer park. Someone who lived in the park tipped us off that every afternoon, three crocodiles swam out of the mangrove swamp and into the creek to sun themselves on a pile of discarded rowboats.

Sure enough, that very afternoon three huge crocodiles looking like snoozing dinosaurs were warming their bellies on the old aluminum boats. This was a great sighting. But we knew that the deeper we went into their world, the more crocodiles we would find. Finding and counting crocodiles in really wild places would be more difficult than it was in the junk-filled creek. Like alligators, crocodiles usually become more active and move about after sundown.

At night, even the shyest crocs leave their hiding places to hunt for food.

But searching around the mangrove swamps looking for crocodiles in the dark was not the safest idea. And because I needed to see the crocodiles well enough to sketch and photograph them, and to capture their movements on video, we decided to do most of our croc hunting during the day. We worked late in the afternoon, when they were just beginning to hunt for food.

Crocodiles will eat anything they can catch, from snakes to waterbirds to raccoons. What they catch most are fish. There is an abundance of fish life in the mangrove swamps.

AMBUSHED FROM BELOW

Alligators stalk their prey, moving closer and closer, until they attack. Crocodiles ambush prey. They find a good place to hide, often submerged underwater, and wait for food to come along.

Crocodiles don't always lunge noisily after their victims, the way you see them do on TV. Sometimes they will slowly rise in the water and quietly pull floating or swimming animals under. We watched a crocodile submerge and then saw this grebe suddenly disappear underwater without so much as a splash!

ONE FAMOUS CROC

This is the crocodile that pulled the grebe under. It was the fourth wild crocodile we found. And it happened to be famous for having migrated hundreds of miles up the coast of Florida from the Everglades to Sanibel Island. The ten-foot-long croc was captured and returned to the Everglades. Then it migrated a second time, all the way back to Sanibel Island, where it remains to this day.

Sanibel Islanders never know where the big croc will show up. We were photographing waterbirds in the island's wildlife refuge when we got to see the huge crocodile completely out of water. It was resting on a long grassy bank with its mouth opened wide to warm its powerful jaw muscles in the sun.

Great Blue Heron

As we watched, the big croc slid into the water and swam slowly, rolling from side to side like a heavy floating log. Most of the animal's massive bulk, including its enormous tail, its huge barrel-shaped body, its thick muscular neck, and its large lower jaw, was completely submerged. Only its eyes and snout and the back of its neck could be seen above the water.

In this way a swimming crocodile, no matter how large, can float near the mangroves and go unnoticed. I was reminded to be extra careful when canoeing close to the small waterside trees.

DANGER UNDERFOOT AND OVERHEAD

In crocodile country, crocodiles aren't the only danger. On the small dry islands called hammocks, diamondback rattlesnakes coil.

When disembarking from our canoe or hiking on trails through the hammocks, we watched every step, knowing we were in rattler habitat.

Along with the venomous snakes, we watched out for poisonwood trees — the bark, wood, sap, and leaves — all of which are highly toxic. Contact with any part of a poisonwood tree can cause a horrible burning of the skin.

It takes a while to learn to recognize poisonwood amid all the other similar gray trees. The key is to look for black blotches on the stems and leaves.

Time: Late afternoon
Weather: Sunny and hot
    following a cold spell

CROCS IN A PILE

Whenever there is a cold spell, reptiles hunker down and suspend activity. Immediately after the cold spell, they come back out in the open to warm up. After two days of cool weather, we traveled to the southernmost tip of the Everglades to see what the return of warm weather might bring.

We counted four large crocodiles sunning themselves on the same mud bank. They had spent the cold days wallowing in muddy water. All four were completely coated. The dry mud coating made them look as if they were sculptured out of the bank itself.

That mud bank must have been the warmest spot around. Three of the four crocs were lying in a pile, all trying to be in the same place at the same time. Such close sharing of the bank led to a few brief jaw-snapping quarrels. One croc had a fresh wound on its snout. But all in all, they shared the sunny spot in peace, and brought our crocodile count to eight.

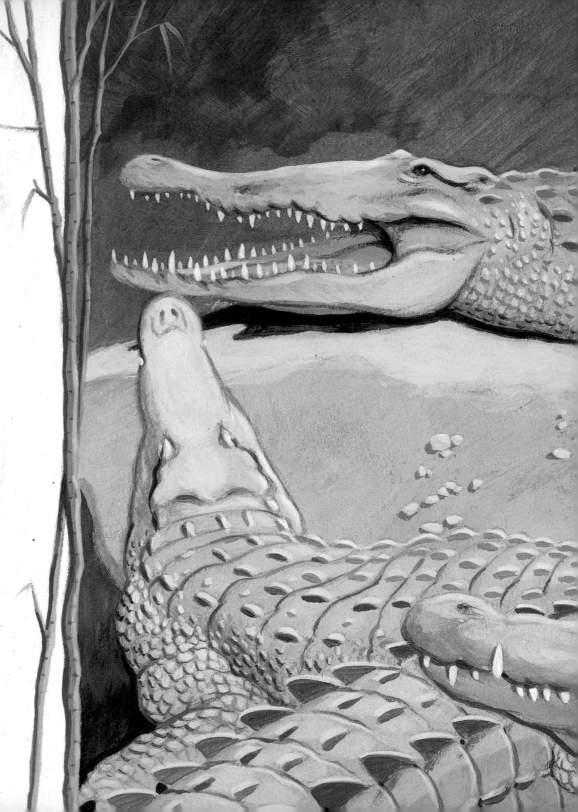

Common Egret

CLOSE ENCOUNTERS

We always kept a safe distance from the crocodiles we saw. Only once did we have a crocodile approach us briefly before it turned and swam away.

Then, one windy day, we canoed past a large crocodile resting on a bank. Its teeth shone brightly in the sun, and I paddled slowly while Deanna videotaped. A sudden gust of wind pushed the canoe toward the croc. I had to paddle harder to keep us from getting too close. Suddenly, the crocodile sprang off the bank into the water, belly flopping loudly just inches from our canoe. It was a startling lesson in just how unpredictable wild animals can be. These two close encounters brought our crocodile count to ten, and also increased the distance we stayed away from the animals.

A crocodile resting its toothy jaws on a waterside stump

CROCODILE TEETH

There are 80 to 120 teeth in a crocodile's mouth. Humans have only 28 to 32 teeth. Some of the croc's teeth are short. Some are long. All are sharply pointed, dense, and incredibly strong. Even so, crocodiles break and lose teeth from time to time, when biting on hard bones and shells. A crocodile can replace lost teeth throughout its life until it becomes so old, it can no longer grow new teeth.

Crocodile teeth shown actual size

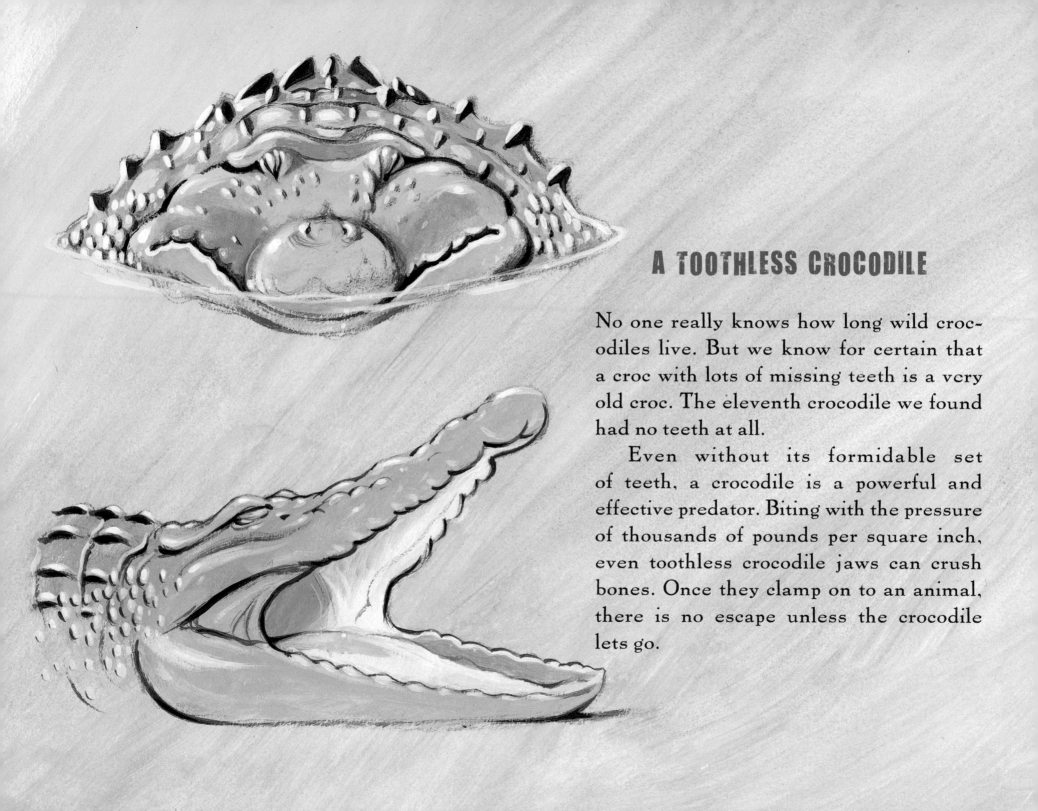

A TOOTHLESS CROCODILE

No one really knows how long wild croc-odiles live. But we know for certain that a croc with lots of missing teeth is a very old croc. The eleventh crocodile we found had no teeth at all.

Even without its formidable set of teeth, a crocodile is a powerful and effective predator. Biting with the pressure of thousands of pounds per square inch, even toothless crocodile jaws can crush bones. Once they clamp on to an animal, there is no escape unless the crocodile lets go.

OUR BIGGEST CROC

All eleven of the crocodiles we had seen were large — eight, nine, ten, and eleven footers. I estimated their sizes in comparison to our twelve-foot canoe. Croc number twelve was longer than our canoe. We saw this clearly because the gigantic reptile emerged and floated in the water close by us. A crocodile longer than twelve feet is a *very* large crocodile. In the U.S., the largest croc on record is fifteen feet in length.

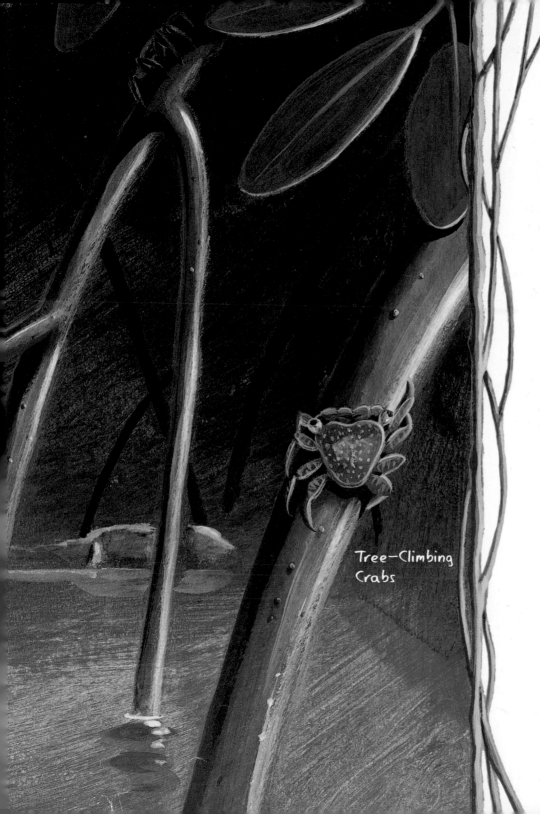

Tree-Climbing
Crabs

Time: Late morning
Weather: Sunlight and shadows
Tide: Receding

SEVEN IN ONE DAY

A great big crocodile is an awesome sight. Yet spotting one floating in the water is not always easy. Crocodiles blend naturally into their surroundings. You can glide right by one in your canoe and not even notice it. Most of the crocodiles we saw were the result of carefully searching the scenery to spot some small part of a croc — a sharply finned tail, ridged back, or blinking crocodile eye.

We hit the jackpot when we located seven crocs in one day, jumping our total count to nineteen. It wasn't because there were suddenly more crocodiles to see. It was that we had just gotten better at seeing them. We saw crocs that were swimming in the water, sunning on floating logs, and crawling slowly on the long mud banks. One well-hidden crocodile eyeballed us cautiously from the shadows behind some mangrove roots.

LIVING WITH DRAGONS

Whenever you look for one animal in the wild, you are sure to find others that share the same habitat. While searching for crocodiles in their natural habitat, we also saw manatees, raccoons, snakes, and lizards, including a few green iguanas descended from the many pet iguanas that have been illegally released in the Everglades.

Large animals, such as manatees and dolphins, had nothing to fear from the huge crocs. Smaller creatures — waterbirds, snakes, raccoons, and lizards — seemed to know when the crocs weren't hungry. During these times, they would get dangerously close to their dragonlike neighbors.

Roseate Spoonbill, Green Iguana, Mangrove Snake, Manatee, and Crocodile

ONE BABY CROCODILE

The last crocodile we counted was this baby who was sunning near a tidal creek on a small bar of bright sand. The little croc was just one foot in length. It was the only baby crocodile that we saw. Where were its nest mates? Were they camouflaged amid the vegetation on the bank? How many more little crocodiles had we paddled by and not seen? What would the official count of U.S. crocodiles be if all the babies could have been seen and counted as easily as this one was?

We had counted twenty wild American crocodiles. The excitement of each sighting remains with us. And with most of their habitat protected, and croc numbers increasing, the thrill of seeing a crocodile in the wild is something we can all look forward to for many years to come.

Counting Crocodiles

Music and lyrics by Jim Arnosky

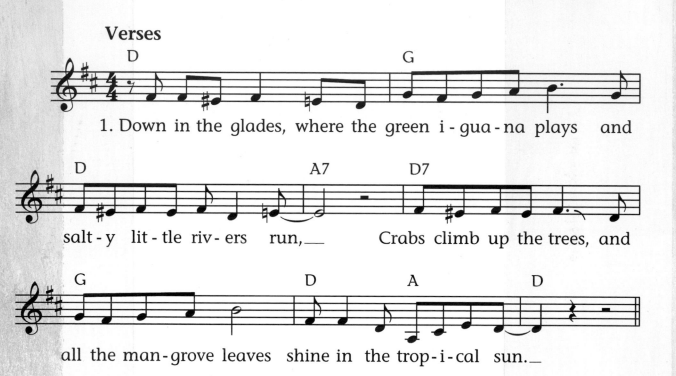

Verses

1. Down in the glades, where the green i - gua - na plays   and

salt - y lit - tle riv - ers   run,___   Crabs climb up the trees, and

all the man - grove leaves shine in the trop - i - cal sun.___

Chorus

It's a place I know where I can al-ways go for ad-
ven-ture and to have a lit-tle fun.__
Float on wa-ter blue in my green can-oe__ Count-ing
croc-o-diles one by one. 2. One

2. One sliding in the water,
   One sunning on a log,
   One crawling on a long mud bank.
   And behind a mangrove root
   I saw one croc who
   Winked at me before she slowly sank.

   Chorus

3. I count ev'ry one
   From the biggest croc on down
   To the babies on their Momma's nest.
   And the tiny toothy smiles
   Of those baby crocodiles
   Are more fun than counting all of the rest.

   *After **Verse 3**,*
   *repeat **Verse 1** and **Chorus**.*

More About Crocodiles

The American crocodile's range includes portions of South America, Central America, Mexico, the Caribbean Islands, and the United States. In the United States, crocodiles are found only in South Florida.

While the American crocodile is no longer considered an endangered species in the United States, it remains an endangered species throughout the rest of its range.

In the United States, the record length of an American crocodile is fifteen feet. In South America, crocodiles grow to be well over twenty feet! The largest crocodiles in the world live on the island of Madagascar in the Indian Ocean and grow to be thirty feet. They are the world's largest living reptiles.

Not all crocodiles worldwide live in salt water. Some, like the Nile River crocodiles in Africa, inhabit freshwater.

The crocodiles counted in the official flyover counts do not include babies, because babies are too small to be seen from an airplane. So, counting babies, there are actually more than 2,000 crocodiles living in the United States.

Crocodiles are dangerous animals, big and powerful enough to pull a deer or a person into the water. Never walk along the water's edge in crocodile areas. And never approach a crocodile, no matter how slow or lazy it appears to be. A crocodile can burst into action and attack very fast for a distance of twenty-five feet.

All the crocodiles Jim and Deanna Arnosky counted were seen in areas of public access where anyone can visit, hike, canoe, and see these magnificent animals for themselves.

CAPTIVA
ISLAND

SANIBEL
ISLAND

KEY
WEST